I'M ADDICTED TO MY CHILDREN

STEPHANIE WILLS

I'm Addicted to My Children

By: Stephanie Wills

I'm Addicted to My Children

Copyright © 2024 by Stephanie Wills

Published by Grace 4 Purpose, Publishing Co. LLC

All rights reserved. No part of this publication may be reproduced in any form or by any electronic or mechanical means, including information storage and retrieval systems, without prior permission in writing from the publisher, except by reviewers, who may quote brief passages in a review.

All scripture quotations, unless otherwise indicated, are taken from the King James Version of the Bible, unless otherwise indicated. All rights reserved.

ISBN: 979-8-9908003-5-9

Editing by: Grace 4 Purpose, Publishing Co. LLC

Book cover design by Grace 4 Purpose, Publishing Co. LLC

Printed and bound in the United States of America

Dedications

This book is dedicated to single mothers and fathers all over the world. Your sacrifice, dedication, and love for your children does not go unnoticed.

I'm Addicted to My Children

A Mother's Love

A mother's love
Her unblemished smile
Her big brown eyes
Her beautiful bronze skin
These are her outer,
let's see what's within

A mother's love is unconditional
Always loving, caring, and childbearing
But most of all, she is always sharing

A mother's love which there is no comparing
God only gave me one mother in this earthly life
To love, honor, and obey
So can you say
You have unconditional love for your mother
In this way

Now take a moment and gaze
At your mother in amaze with appraise
Nowadays you won't find another
To love like your mother

Her unblemished smile
Her big brown eyes
Her beautiful bronze skin
These are all outer
Now you know what's within

- Stephanie Wills (Poems of the Nile)

TABLE OF CONTENTS

Introduction..…..................5
Chapter One..…..............11
Chapter Two...…..........22
Chapter Three...….......33
Chapter Four..…......39
Chapter Five...….....45
Chapter Six..…....51
Chapter Seven...….....56
About the Author..……......60

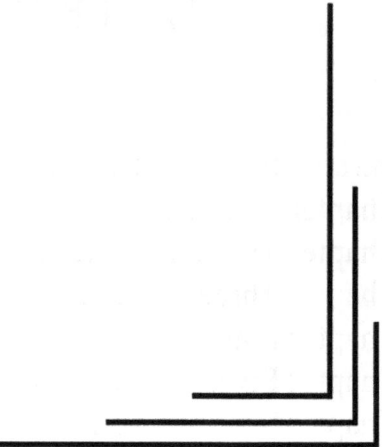

Introduction

> "AND, YE FATHERS, PROVOKE NOT YOUR CHILDREN TO WRATH: BUT BRING THEM UP IN THE NURTURE AND ADMONITION OF THE LORD."
>
> **EPHESIANS 6:4**

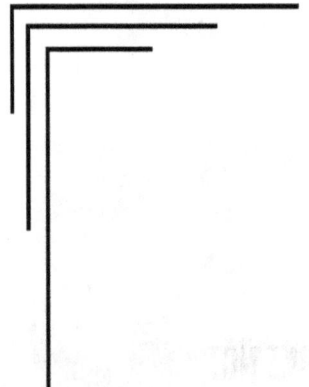

Introduction

"And, ye fathers, provoke not your children to wrath: but bring them up in the nurture and admonition of the Lord."
-Ephesians 6:4

Welcome to my unique way of thinking. I'm sure many of you have gone through similar experiences that I am going to share in your own upbringing and with raising your children. It doesn't matter if your children are young or old, we as parents may find ourselves involved in our children's lives with no balance. Our intentions are never to harm them but to help them make wise decisions.

I'm Addicted to My Children

The journey that I am going to share with you is my addiction to my own children and how I had to learn to find balance. I have three children, a son and two daughters. I have been a single mom raising my three beautiful and very unique children who are now adults. Their ages are twenty-five, thirty-four and thirty-six years old. Before I share about my journey as a mother, I want to give you a little insight into my own upbringing with my parents. I have learned over time that everything is connected to my experiences as I was growing up. My experiences impacted the way that I raised my children.

I lived in a home with my four older siblings, my mom and dad. My parents were very different in their parenting styles, one was soft and the other was hard. You can decide which one was hard and which one was soft as we continue. My mother worked for a while, then she became a housewife. My dad worked for the gas company for many years until he became sick. My dad would wake me up very early for school, not my brothers and sisters, just me. I always wondered why he treated me differently than my other siblings growing up, I didn't understand until later in life. Mom would pack our lunch, give us a kiss and send us on our way. My dad drove me as close as he could to school because it was close to his job. There was a breakfast place that we used to visit before we went our separate ways for the day. The funny thing is my dad never allowed me to eat meat for breakfast, only grits, eggs, and toast. Ironically, he enjoyed eating meat for breakfast, I never understood why I couldn't have it and it's one of those things I never asked about.

They both had their own special way of dealing with all of us. I won't go in too deep into my childhood, but there are some things I want to share so that you can see why I am addicted to my children.

My dad was very tough, and my mom was very soft and sweet, always ready to hear what we had to say. Whatever we were going through she would give us advice. Mom and I were more like friends as I was growing up. I loved it, but as I got older things changed, I was no longer a baby girl, I was grown. I always knew that I was different than my siblings. They had a different personality, they were more outspoken and had lots of friends. As for me, I was very quiet and close to my mom. I looked at my dad differently, he was very stern, and he did not play games with us. He and mom wanted nothing but the best for all of us. However, we were all different in our own way and the way that my dad treated me versus how he treated my siblings would be something I'll never forget.

I always felt like I had to prove myself to my father growing up, he always challenged me to go the extra mile. I always felt as though my effort was not good enough. As I got older, I asked my father why he was harder on me and not the rest of my siblings. He stated because he knew I would have to be stronger later in life. As a child, I needed my dad the same way that my siblings did. Just because I appeared stronger didn't mean that I didn't need to feel his compassion. I was still his little girl. I never got to experience that "daddies' little girl" feeling.

I knew before I even had children of my own that I would never treat them the way that I was treated growing up. My children would always know that I was there for them and that they didn't have to figure out life alone. In hindsight, my relationship with my father may have had some influence on the addiction I have to my children. I never wanted them to feel alone in this world.

> CHILDREN ARE A HERITAGE FROM THE LORD, OFFSPRING A REWARD FROM HIM.
>
> **-PSALM 127:3 (KJV)**

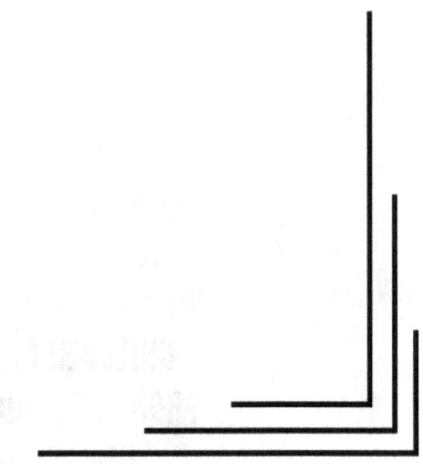

Chapter One

"So do not fear, for I am with you; do not be dismayed, for I am your God. I will strengthen you and help you; I will uphold you with my righteous right hand."

-Isaiah 41:10 (NIV)

It was a cold winter day, one in which my bed felt so comfortable as I was laying under my warm blankets. My alarm went off and I pushed the snooze button because I truly just wanted to stay home and relax, but I knew that was not going to happen. So, after a few more turns and stretches under the warm blankets, I pushed myself up and got ready for the day. When I rose up and put my legs on the side of the bed, I felt a small pain in my stomach and my bladder felt very full. I never had that happen before so I stood up and began to walk into the bathroom and I sat down on the toilet. I felt some pain and I started feeling very nauseous. I began getting dress for the day, still unsure as to why my stomach was in pain or why I was feeling nauseous. Nevertheless, I called my job and explained to them that I needed to go to the Hospital. I tried calling some of my friends to see who would be able to accompany me, but I had no luck, everyone was busy.

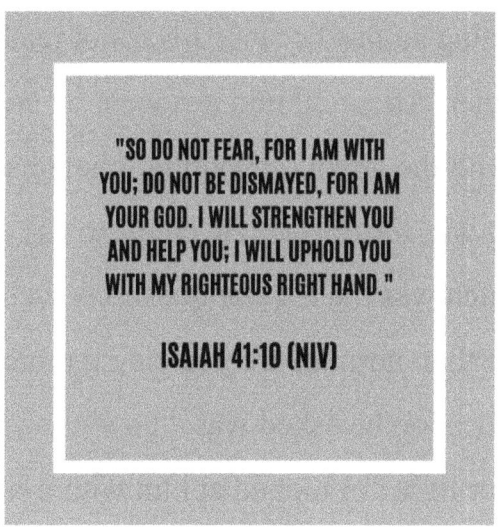

I ended up just driving myself to the hospital, this pain I was feeling wasn't normal. I couldn't wait any longer. Once I arrived at the hospital they started the normal process of checking all of my vitals. The nurse asked me when was my last menstrual, I told her that my cycle is regular and in fact it just went off. I never missed a month. She said, "Okay", and then walked out the room and told me to get undressed. About ten minutes went by before the nurse came in and asked me if by any chance could I be pregnant. I laughed and said, "Not at all, I am on the pill and I never miss a beat." Then she looked at me with a smile on her face and stated, "I will be right back." Listen, at this moment, my heart was beating so fast because I was not ready to be anyone's mother. About 20 minutes went by and I was still in the room with the gown on waiting. I heard a soft knock on the door, it was the doctor. He began to ask me several questions, which was the regular questions such as, "are you sleeping more than normal, are you eating more or less," and the last question he asked was, "how was your last cycle was it heavy or light?" I looked at him with a smile on my face and said, "Sir, please don't play with me. I am not having any babies no time soon." He continued on with his questions and trying to get a better understanding of why I was there. He asked me to lay back so that he can begin the examination so I did. The exam didn't take long at all. He said, "I am done", he went over to the sink and began to wash his hands. Once he was finished, he walked to the door and said I could get dressed and he would be back. He didn't mention that he saw or felt anything out of the ordinary, so I thought that maybe it was nothing wrong. I heard that soft knock on the door again asking if I was dressed and if it was okay to come in. The doctor and nurse came in the room together, she was standing there with a computer in her hand.

Once the doctor began talking to me, I noticed the nurse typing on her computer. I immediately started to feel like something was up. My heart began to race really fast. I asked the doctor what's going on? He sat on the little black stool; my palms were wet due to my nerves. I looked at him and say well, he asked if I had any children and I said, "No, why?" I took a deep breath. He told me that I was three months pregnant. Tears started to stream down my face. I wasn't sad, just surprised. When I left the hospital I called my husband and told him what the doctor said. He was super happy. After nine months' out came my first baby, a handsome son; it was a beautiful, unexpected experience.

My journey did not end there. Two years after having my son I found out that I was having another baby; and boy was I nervous. This pregnancy was quite different, my first pregnancy was planned and this second pregnancy came as a surprise. I also had my son two weeks after my due date, however, my daughter arrived a month early. When I was pregnant with my son, my stomach was very big and round, I did not feel cute at all. The second pregnancy while carrying my daughter, my stomach was so small and very cute, and I carried her low. Also, all I wanted to do is eat chicken day and night. The sad part about this go around is that I knew I would be raising my kids alone. My husband and I started to have some issues with one another at that time. Nevertheless, I gave birth to a beautiful little girl. Her eyes were so bright, and her smile would light up a room. She was a happy little princess.

Years later I adopted a beautiful little girl, she was a picture-perfect baby. She never liked to eat. All she wanted was her bottle and her stuffed animal. As my journey continued, my children reached the age in which they were more independent. Meaning they did not need me as much; they moved out of my house and into their own place. They had their own children and significant others. So, I began stepping back from them, but honestly it really hurt my feelings. The feelings I had was jealousy than anything because in my mind, no one can take care of them but me.

My heart would not accept the fact that they are grown. I am addicted to my children on a higher level. How do I get pass this stage in my life. Only one thing came to my mind, I must trust God and let them go before it's too late. God reminded me that I have done my part and that I needed to trust Him and let Him take over. This was not going to be easy.

This second part of my journey was not easy, but it started to get a little more comfortable over time because I decided to let God take the lead. How did it make me feel you ask? A bit nervous, but I knew God would send His Angels to keep watch over my children.

One day I was sitting and staring out the window, watching the rain fall. Tears began to fill my eyes, and I felt so alone because my kids did not need my help anymore. They were taking family trips with their kids, and I was left taking care of their dogs. I was very sad and there was nothing I could do about it but respect their choice. Ironically, my daughter called and said she did not feel well. My heart dropped to the floor. How can I get to her and I have the baby and the dog here with me? My business is still open, I started to panic. After taking a few deep breaths, I decided to reach back out to her by way of a text giving her some instructions of what to buy from a drug store. She replied, "Mom I got this, please don't worry my friends are taking good care of me." My response to her was, "Don't play with me, I will get a plane ticket and come right where you are with no problem." She laughed and told me to calm down and reassured me that everything was going to be okay. This wasn't the first time and it definitely would not be the last that I began to panic almost immediately at the first thought of something being wrong with one of my kids.

Listen, please understand when you are a parent there is no book out there in which would tell you step by step on how to be a great mom. We must walk by faith and not by sight. Remember, God our father will protect each and every one of us. Our job is to listen for the sweet and soft voice to guide us each step of the way. Remember this if nothing else, your children, young and old will always be your children, and when they grow older they will remember everything that you have imparted within them. Our job as parents and believers is to learn to speak the truth and be the best example that we can be to our children. We can do this by following the instructions the Lord gives each and every one of His children, in His Word.

As you continue to read about my journey, you must have a clear understanding of what the word addiction means. The word addiction means to be physically and mentally dependent on a particular substance, and unable to stop taking it without incurring adverse effects. Addictions can feel like a form of bondage. That bondage can make you feel as though you are trapped in your mind, which makes it very difficult to handle transitions and accept certain truths. Those struggling with addiction are often viewed as a failure, weak, or insignificant.

My struggle with addiction is very different than what you may think when you hear that word. My addiction is connected to my children and the anxiety that can onset when I am not around them or able to communicate with them. As you read about my journey, I ask that you read with an open mind, and also with an open heart.

> "TRUST IN THE LORD WITH ALL YOUR HEART AND LEAN NOT ON YOUR OWN UNDERSTANDING; IN ALL YOUR WAYS SUBMIT TO HIM, AND HE WILL MAKE YOUR PATHS STRAIGHT."
>
> —PROVERBS 3:5-6 (NIV)

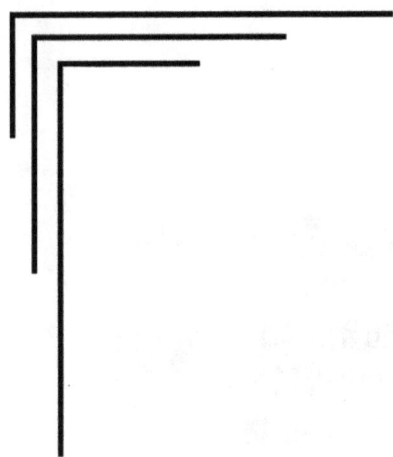

Chapter Two

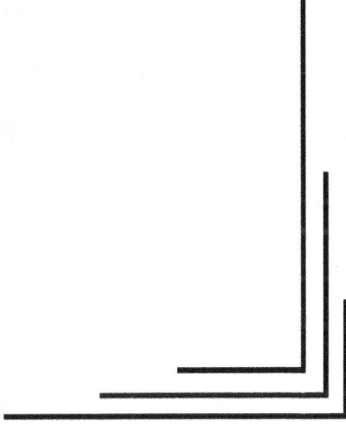

Chapter Two

"Children, obey your parents in the Lord: for this is right. Honour thy father and mother; which is the first commandment with promise;
That it may be well with thee, and thou mayest live long on the earth.
And, ye fathers, provoke not your children to wrath: but bring them up in the nurture and admonition of the Lord."
-Ephesians 6:1-4

I was 23 years old and had only been married for just a few years when I had my first child. My first born was my son, he was so handsome, quiet, loved to eat and very smart. My son and I were very close, although I was married, it seemed like it was just him and I for two years. We did everything together from shopping, going to the movies, out to eat and more. Anything you can think of we did it, until one day I made the decision to enroll him in daycare. I started working at Campbell Soup, so of course I could not take my son to work with me. I also wanted him to get the experience of being around other children outside of the house. Everything seemed to be going okay at first. It was a big adjustment with me dropping him off every day, he was so used to being with me.

He eventually got comfortable with the drop offs and didn't cry as I was leaving. I started to feel pretty secure about leaving him at daycare while I was at work, until two weeks later he was involved in a bad accident. When I arrived at the daycare he had a big lump in the middle of his head. He was crying and so was I. I remember telling him that I would never let anybody hurt him again. From that day on, I kept him with me everywhere I went. I never let him go back to that daycare center or any other daycare after that. Due to developing a medical condition called carpel tunnel. I had to stop working anyway, so there really was no point in me placing him back in daycare. I eventually started my own in-home daycare and the rest is history.

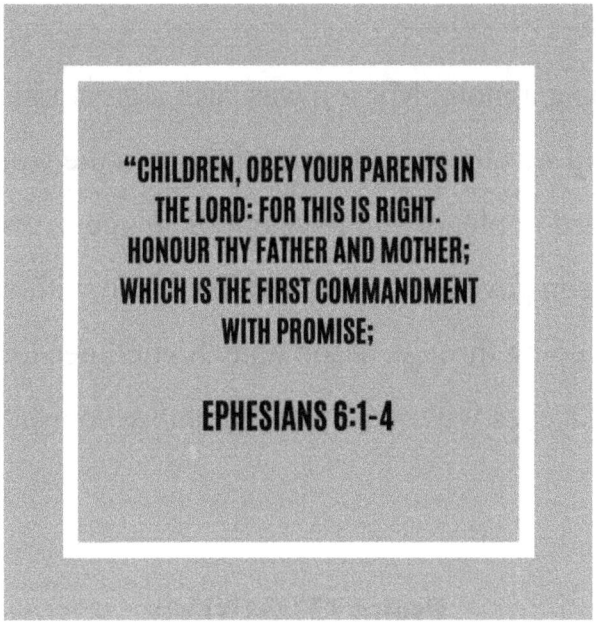

As he got older, he was introduced to football and Karate. He was participating in both activities and had a great experience. He decided he wanted to play football and not do karate anymore. He made it all the way to his next belt which was-black belt. Nevertheless, it was fine with me because he was in the process of discovering what he enjoyed. **Parents, it is important that we give our children**

opportunities to try new things, that is the only way they will be able to discover what they like.

I loved being a mom. My son was such a great kid. Our relationship was the most beautiful thing in the world. He was not hard to please and gave out the biggest, warmest hugs. My son gave me a reason to live, even with everything that I was going through at the time. Sometimes looking into your child's eyes will make you remember your purpose for living.

Psalm 127:3 (NIV):
"Children are a heritage from the Lord, offspring a reward from him.

Time went on and before I knew it, I was pregnant again two years later. This time I had a beautiful daughter. She was so beautiful, very smart, and very creative. I was overprotective of her as well. My son and daughter were different. It took a lot for me to get my son to open up about things. For example, if I asked him, how his day went, he would just say one word; that drove me crazy. When I would ask my daughter how her day was, she went on and on to the point where I had to tell her to slow down.

It was just the three of us until my youngest daughter came into our lives. She lived with us on and off for a few years because I was her foster mom. I had the pleasure of adopting her when she was three years old. My youngest daughter was different from my oldest daughter. I had to learn a lot about her in order to help her. She was a very smart and creative little girl. As time went on I started to notice different things. There were times when she would refuse to eat and would just sit at the dinner table. She had a different diet at her prior living arrangements, a soft diet. It took some time to get her adjusted to eating habits that would be best for her growth. Not only did she have to adjust to her new surroundings and way of living, but my older children also had to adjust to her living with us. She used to go into my oldest daughter's room and just start screaming without any explanation. Her older sister would kick her out of her room whenever she started doing that. It was an adjustment for everyone, but over time we found our balance.

As my children started to get older and have their own lives, I started to notice that I did not have much balance. It was hard for me to let go of them being around me all the time. I started to notice first with my son that I had an addiction to my children. When my son moved out, I would call him excessively, so he stopped answering my calls. Not talking to him put me in a place I did not know how to handle. I found myself going to his house if he did not answer my text or my calls. I started to realize that I had turned into a worrying mom.

As my son got older, he brought two beautiful daughters into this world. Whenever he was in trouble or just needed money for his apartment or anything, I was always right there. There was no limit on how much they needed or wanted. I gave everything I had to make sure they didn't have to want for anything.

> **4 LOVE IS PATIENT, LOVE IS KIND. IT DOES NOT ENVY, IT DOES NOT BOAST, IT IS NOT PROUD. 5 IT DOES NOT DISHONOR OTHERS, IT IS NOT SELF-SEEKING, IT IS NOT EASILY ANGERED, IT KEEPS NO RECORD OF WRONGS. 6 LOVE DOES NOT DELIGHT IN EVIL BUT REJOICES WITH THE TRUTH. 7 IT ALWAYS PROTECTS, ALWAYS TRUSTS, ALWAYS HOPES, ALWAYS PERSEVERES.**
>
> **(1ST CORINTHIANS 13:4-7)**

He met another young lady, and they got married. In the Bible in Genesis 2:24, it reminded me that I have to let him go and he has to cling to his wife. This was very hard for me, letting go and giving him the space to now build a new life as a husband. The text messages saying, "mommy I love you", the coming over, and bringing the kids to me, all of these things stopped to a certain degree. I thought that over time it was going to get easier, but it did not get any better. I would call him and he did not answer. My heart would beat so fast and I would get so stressed out. I would get in my car and drive to his house and knock on the door and ask him, "Why did you not answer my calls or my texts? Is everything OK?" He would look at me and say, "Mom I love you, but you have to calm down. We are fine here." I couldn't do anything but walk away and say, "ok". When I reached the bottom steps of his house, I would turn around and say to him, "Don't play with me boy, I love you and I don't want anything to happen to you. Do you understand?" My son would look at me and say, "Yes ma'am, but we are all OK. Stop worrying." This routine would happen more times than I care to admit.

^{4} Love is patient, love is kind. It does not envy, it does not boast, it is not proud. ^{5} It does not dishonor others, it is not self-seeking, it is not easily angered, it keeps no record of wrongs. ^{6} Love does not delight in evil but rejoices with the truth. ^{7} It always protects, always trusts, always hopes, always perseveres.
(1st Corinthians 13:4-7)

My son and I have many similarities in the way that we felt growing up, I felt misunderstood, and he did too. He thought that he had no voice, I always tried to encourage him to learn to speak up in a decent and orderly manner. Now that he is a parent, he is facing some challenges. Some of the things that I was trying to prepare him for, he is having his own experiences and test that he is going through. He is beginning to understand that I was not trying to control him, I was trying to prepare him.

> "ALL YOUR CHILDREN WILL BE TAUGHT BY THE LORD, AND GREAT WILL BE THEIR PEACE."
>
> —ISAIAH 54:13 (NIV)

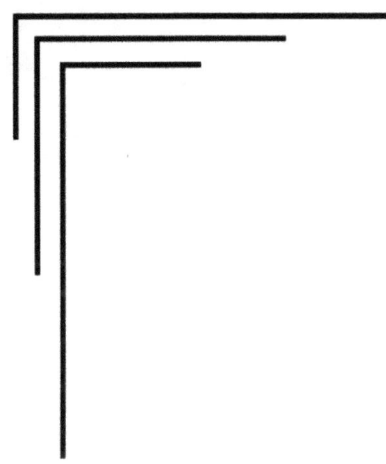

Chapter Three

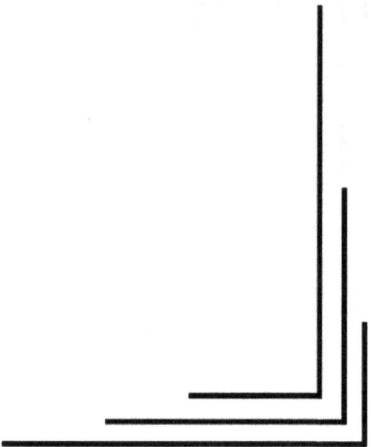

Chapter Three

Train up a child in the way he should go: and when he is old, he will not depart from it.
-Proverbs 22:6

My oldest daughter has always been my rock, she never experienced having to go to an outside daycare because I started doing in-home daycare. She has been by my side since she was younger and even now. There are reasons that I was protective of my daughters that were different than my son. When I was growing up there were some bad things that happened to me that made me be who I am today; very,

very overprotective of my children. The relationship I have with my older daughter is great, as she has gotten older we have become more like friends, but of course we have those boundaries established where she knows that I am the mom. She now has someone in her life that loves her and wants to be with her.

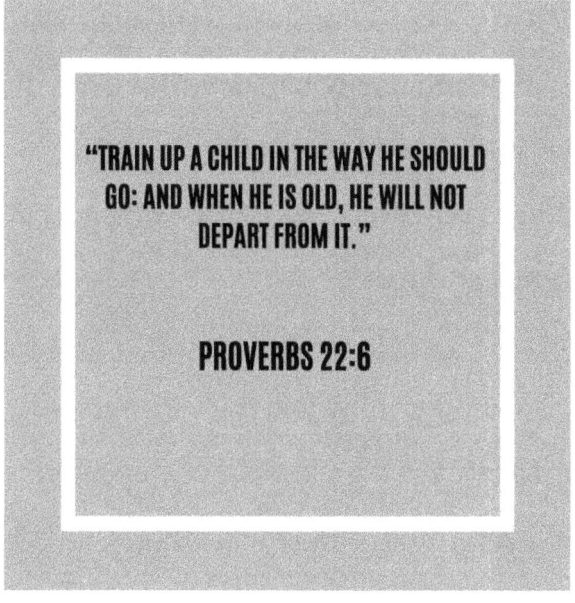

"TRAIN UP A CHILD IN THE WAY HE SHOULD GO: AND WHEN HE IS OLD, HE WILL NOT DEPART FROM IT."

PROVERBS 22:6

I remember praying about this because I wanted her to be happy and treated like the queen that she is. Although our relationship has been pretty great and we can talk about everything, I still had to learn how to break away from the addiction that I had to my children.

My oldest daughter left home at 18, although I was happy for her, I worried about her. This was a challenge for me, because I was overprotective so it was hard to let her go. However, I knew that if I didn't give her space to learn and grow on her own, it could create a wedge in our relationship. Over time we created a new balance with her being out on her own. We still have a great bond. Her being in a relationship does not affect the bond we have established if anything it grew stronger.

Seeing her as a mother now and how she raises her son, it amazes me. They have a great relationship and they are able to talk about everything, and that is always what I wanted with my children. I can see where some of those things I instilled in her have stuck in the way that she raises her son.

One thing that parents should understand that each child is different and the way that they need to be nurtured may be different. I learned that with my son, he pulled away when I tried to get too close when he was an adult. My oldest daughter, she needed my nurturing more, so she did not pull away from my tendency to be a little close. My youngest daughter, well our experience was very different.

My children sometimes feel as though I am doing too much and I'm not allowing them to grow and make their own mistakes. In my eyes I felt like I was doing the right thing keeping them safe and warning them of things that I've seen or may have heard. My intentions are always in their best interest, I just had to learn through experience what worked for each of them differently and break the habit of being addicted to them.

> "THESE COMMANDMENTS THAT I GIVE YOU TODAY ARE TO BE ON YOUR HEARTS. IMPRESS THEM ON YOUR CHILDREN. TALK ABOUT THEM WHEN YOU SIT AT HOME AND WHEN YOU WALK ALONG THE ROAD, WHEN YOU LIE DOWN AND WHEN YOU GET UP."
>
> **-DEUTERONOMY 6:6-7 (NIV)**

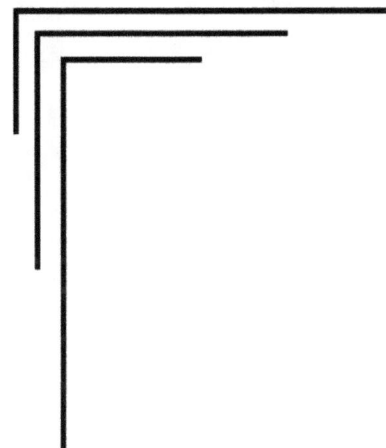

Chapter Four

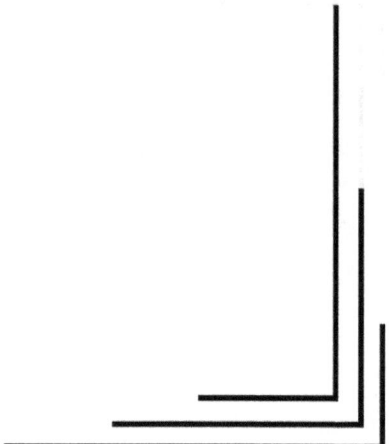

Chapter Four

"learn to do good; seek justice, correct oppression; bring justice to the fatherless, plead the widow's cause."

-Isaiah 1:17

I was a foster mom to many children and had the wisdom to deal with different personalities and differing backgrounds. I started doing foster care around the same time that I started doing daycare, fostering at least 50-60 children. I would take on emergency cases, long-term cases, overnight respite care and more. Although I cared for a lot of foster children, there was only one child that I adopted. There were other children that I tried to adopt throughout the years, but the system was not set up for me to adopt them. The system was set up for reunification with the children's biological parents.

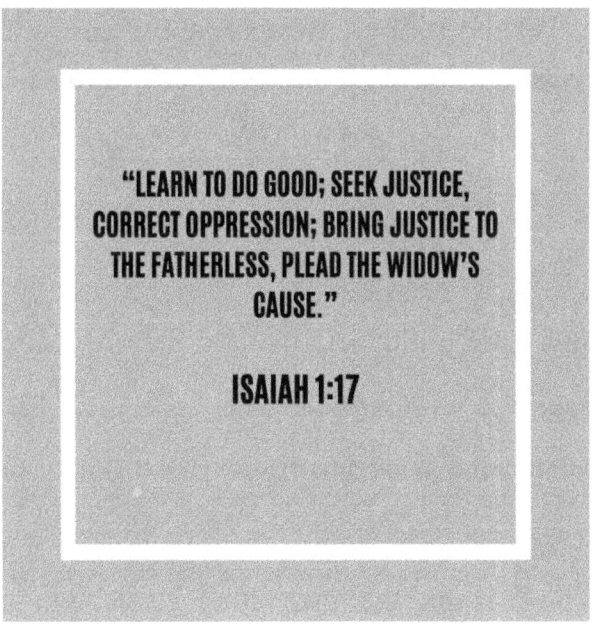

Nonetheless, I took on the new responsibility of being an adopted mother to my youngest daughter to heart. I knew that it would take time and patience to build a relationship with my youngest daughter. When she first came into my life she came from a different upbringing than how I was raising my two children. I was her foster mother first and then adopted her at three years old.

"Religion that God our Father accepts as pure and faultless is this: to look after orphans and widows in their distress and to keep oneself from being polluted by the world."

James 1:27 (NIV):

There came a time in our relationship that my adopted daughter began to wonder where her biological parents were. We went on a search to find her biological parents. Our search was successful and we were able to find her mother's side first and then her father's side. This is one of the great memories that we share.

Although my youngest daughter is adopted I still have unconditional love for her and there is nothing that I would not do for her; the same as my other two children. As she got older she made the decision to live the life that she chose, which created distance and caused our conversations to be limited. That doesn't mean that I don't worry about her constantly or want to check in on her, but at some point you have to allow your children to find their own way.

Like the story of the prodigal son in the Bible, children always return back home. We just have to continue praying and have open arms for them when they come back; just as God has for us.

> "A FATHER TO THE FATHERLESS, A DEFENDER OF WIDOWS, IS GOD IN HIS HOLY DWELLING. GOD SETS THE LONELY IN FAMILIES, HE LEADS OUT THE PRISONERS WITH SINGING; BUT THE REBELLIOUS LIVE IN A SUN-SCORCHED LAND."
>
> -PSALM 68:5-6 (NIV)

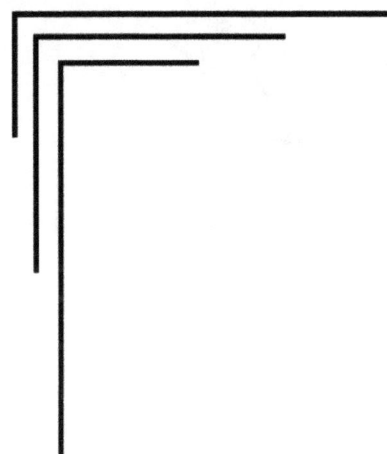

Chapter Five

Chapter Five

"Where there is no guidance, a people falls, but in an abundance of counselors there is safety"

-Proverbs 11:14

I reached out to a counselor for help because I thought I had everything figured out. I never saw this as an addiction, just a mom who loves her children and would do anything to put a smile on their face. I didn't want them to struggle or be sad. My behavior became a big problem. I could not sleep, eat, or breathe until I heard their voice saying good night mom. I'm still working on pushing back and allowing them to raise their children the way they see fit. Being a parent takes a lot of faith and trust in them as well as myself. My job is to sit back and watch how they raise their kids without budding in. Although it is tough for me, I am trying to stay out of their way and trust that I have given them enough guidance that they will lead their own children the right way. I remember crying, praying, and asking God to help me be strong as I tried to give them the space they needed to build their own families.

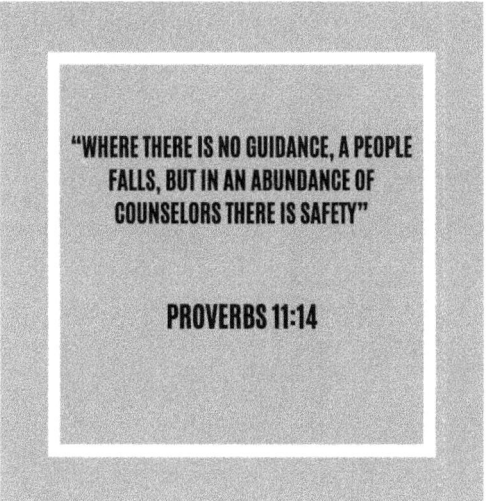

One thing that helped me to stay strong and encouraged is when I read the scripture that talked about seeking good counsel. Proverbs1:5: "A wise man will hear and will increase learning; and a man of understanding shall attain unto wise counsels." Counseling was helpful and to this day I still reach out to my counselor a few times a week if necessary. Although, I do believe that counseling is a great resource, I can't ignore how important it is to listen to that silent voice that is always with us. The voice of the Lord. His voice has really helped me to navigate this new season of my life. As I am learning to give my children the space and grace that they need to be parents, I am reminded that it truly does take a village to raise a child. I now have the opportunity to support my children in a different way, as a grandmother.

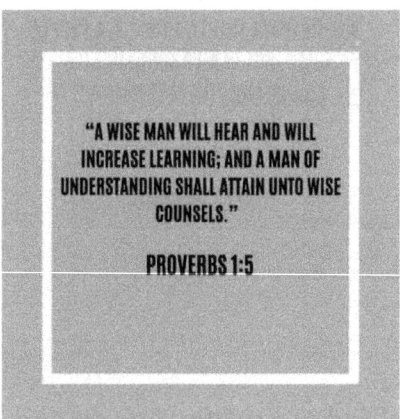

Single parents, you may think that you can figure things out alone or even say things like, "I got this", or "I don't need anyone to help me raise my child/ren". God gave you a village for a reason. Give your parents the opportunity to support you the best way that they know how.

This journey is what I like to call a forever adventure. Parenting doesn't stop just because your children have turned 18 years old, it doesn't stop when they move out of the house and on their own. It doesn't even stop when they have children of their own. The struggle that I have had with backing away from my children and giving them the space to grow has not been easy. There have been times where I feel that the love I have for them, the need to have that constant communication with them for my own peace of mind has caused more damage than good.

As your children get older, they get into relationships, get married and have families of their own. If your experience has been anything like mine, you may understand how difficult it is to let them go as they create new lives with their significant other.

> "IF ANY OF YOU LACKS WISDOM, LET HIM ASK OF GOD, WHO GIVES TO ALL LIBERALLY AND WITHOUT REPROACH, AND IT WILL BE GIVEN TO HIM."
>
> —JAMES 1:5 (NIV)

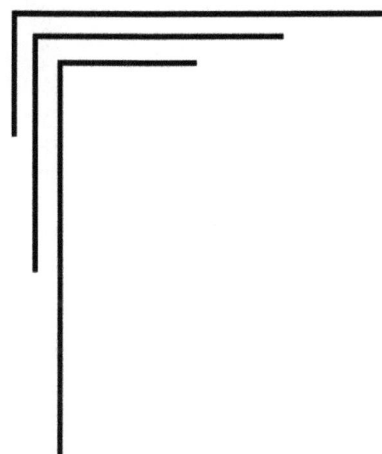

Chapter Six

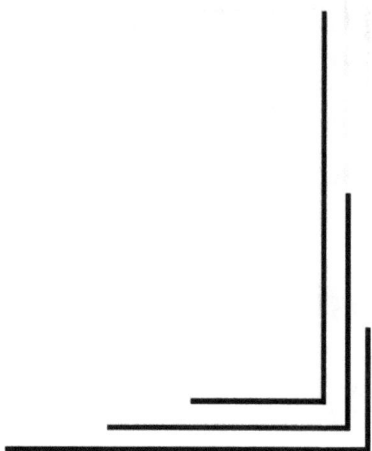

Chapter Six

"Train up a child in the way he should go, And when he is old he will not depart from it."

-Proverbs- 22:6

Time has progressed for me, and all of my children are now adults with their own families. I am now learning how to parent adult children with children. My stepping back and allowing my children to learn and grow on their own has created a new voice without judgement. I no longer have to worry about not hearing from them or not seeing them, they now take the initiative on their own.

As my children have gotten older, they have reminded me of the great job that I did raising them. Even through the hardships, disappointments, misunderstandings, and those times I doubted myself, I can see where the prayers I prayed were not in vain. My children want me to be able to live my life and be happy.

Although, things are starting to get better and I am learning to balance my role as a mom and a grandmother now, I am still working through the journey of releasing the addiction that I have to my children. Over time I have learned, I am just a mother who cares deeply about the well-being of my children, and now my grandchildren. So, where some may call it an addiction, or clingy or overbearing, I am just a mother who will never stop praying and never stop showing that AGAPE love.

As the days go on I feel like I am making progress. It is getting easier every day; I am praying to God for more wisdom and understanding. In my prayers I ask God to watch over each and every one of my children.

> "BEING CONFIDENT OF THIS, THAT HE WHO BEGAN A GOOD WORK IN YOU WILL CARRY IT ON TO COMPLETION UNTIL THE DAY OF CHRIST JESUS."
>
> -PHILIPPIANS 1:6 (NIV)

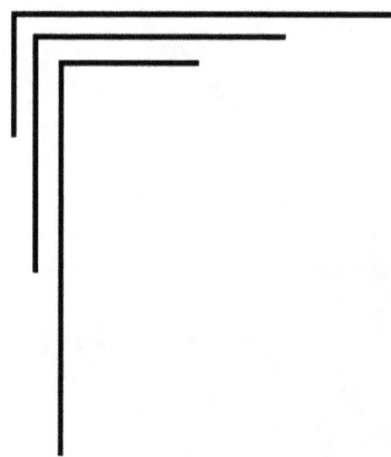

Chapter Seven

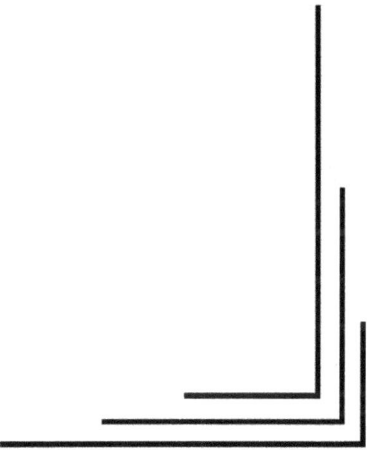

Chapter Seven

"And these words, which I command thee this day, shall be in thine heart: And thou shalt teach them diligently unto thy children, and shalt talk of them when thou sittest in thine house, and when thou walkest by the way, and when thou liest down, and when thou risest up."

-Deuteronomy 6:6-7

There has been so much that I have been able to discover about myself during this part of my journey. While I am still a work in progress, and still have those moments where I am constantly worrying about my children and wanting to call, text or drive to their house if I don't hear from them, I am learning patience.

Now that my children are older and building their own families, I am learning that it is okay to focus on the things that I enjoy doing. I had to relearn this because much of my time and energy was focused on worrying about my children and constantly wanting to check in on them. I didn't realize how deep into this I really was.

I am really seeking God for this next chapter and he is reminding me to brush the dust off of some of those gifts I laid aside. I have found time to really start focus on things that I enjoy doing like, helping others get closer to God, and writing song lyrics.

I would encourage all parents that reach this part of their journey to do these three things:

1. **Be patient** during your journey and keep your mind on the Word of God.

2. **Never stop talking**, always have a "never give up" spirit throughout your journey.

3. Lastly, know that **you're not alone** but remember you are a mother every day and nothing shall shock or move you with the love of God. Stay focused and faithful to His Word.

No matter how old your children may get, always have a shoulder for them to lean on, and a lap to sit on. Encourage them as God has always been there for us. We need to be there for our children. Never stop praying for and covering your children. Remember, they are a work in progress and still need grace to grow and learn; even as adults.

Heavenly Father,

I thank you for this amazing day, a day of opportunity to give someone a special token of love. I thank you for all you have brought me through. I thank you for eyes to see and ears to hear. I thank you, Lord God for everything that you have taught me as a parent. Father God, you taught me how to love my children unconditionally. You taught me how to walk in your path that you have laid down before me as a mom. You reminded me that your Word doesn't come back void. Father God, you said to continue to pray for them and to keep watch over each and every one of them to the best of my ability. So let it be said, so it can be done, in Jesus name,

Amen

About the Author

Stephanie Wills was born in 1962, the fifth child of five to Mr. and Mrs. Weldon Johnson. Stephanie's passion for writing started at the age of five where she wrote many fantasy stories as a child. In her spare time she enjoys taking care of her children, swimming, bowling, and traveling.

As years went by, her dream and vision of owning a daycare center became a reality. She has been up and operating now for forty-four years. This was just one. Of the many great accomplishments that she has achieved. As Stephanie continues with her passion for writing she has now completed four inspirational books, Phases of life, The Road to Emotional Healing, and Flowing Waters Presents: Poems of the Nile (First and Second Edition). She currently resides in Philadelphia, PA.

Contact the Author

Email: willstr@aol.com

I'm Addicted to My Children

www.grace4purposeco.com

www.ingramcontent.com/pod-product-compliance
Lightning Source LLC
Chambersburg PA
CBHW060031180426
43196CB00044B/2467